Consilience Series

CENTRE AND CIRCUMFERENCE: A COLLECTION OF POEMS

by Howard F. Stein

LOVE and LIFE

TIME and MEMORIES

WORK and SOCIETY

Published in 2017 by
MindMend Publishing, New York, NY

Copyright © 2017 by Howard F. Stein, PhD

All rights reserved.

For permissions to reproduce any part of this publication, email to ORIPressEditor@Gmail.com or write to ORI Academic Press/ MindMend Publishing Editor @ 7515 187th St, Fresh Meadows, NY 11366.

Printed in the United States of America on acid free paper.

Cataloging Data

Stein, Howard F. *Centre and Circumference: A Collection of Poems* / Howard F. Stein. [Consilience Series]

1. Poetry. 2. Psychobiography. 3. Psychohistory. 4. History and criticism. 5. Conscious and unconscious communications.
6. Creativity (literary, artistic, etc.) – Psychological concepts.

Library of Congress Control Number: 2018934100

ISBN-13: 978-1-942431-09-1 (soft cover)

Artwork Copyright © by Sandra Indig @ www.sindig.com

Book design, editing, and book cover art –
by MindMendMedia, Inc. @ MindMendMedia.com

To Johanna Shapiro, PhD,

with

gratitude,

admiration,

and affection

TABLE OF CONTENTS

ACKNOWLEDGEMENTS xi

FOREWORD xiii

INTRODUCTION xvii

LOVE AND LIFE

Companionship 3
Embraces 5
Unanswered Questions 6
Nothing 7
Tweet and Text 9
Planetary 10
Once 11
Metric 12
Crescendo 13
Disappointment 14
What's Left 15
Hands 16
Liebeslieder Gedichte, Love Song Poems 17
The Reach 19
Purpose 20
Gemütlich / Gemütlichkeit 21
The Wall 22
Filament 23
Loneliness 24
Ice 25
A Splash of Cold Water 27
Prize Song, after Wagner 28
Arithmetic 29

Contradictions 30
Flaw 31
Character 32
Defiance 33
Pacing 35
After You Died 36
Conventions 37
The Cellist 38

TIME AND MEMORIES

Visit to a Clock Repair Shop 43
Keys 44
Palpable 45
At the Art Exhibit 46
Dedication 47
Uncle Hymen 49
Pressed Leaf 51
Mesas and Meadows, Ghost Ranch, NM 52
Sovereignty in the Mesas, Ghost Ranch, NM 53
Inanimate, But Not Dead, Ghost Ranch, NM 55
Bristlecone Pine, Great Basin 56
Leaving Ghost Ranch, NM 57
High Desert Valley, Ghost Ranch, NM 58
Mesas and Mountains, Ghost Ranch, NM 59
It Goes Either Way 60
Seeing Twice 61
Invitation to the Dance 62
Filling in, Ghost Ranch, NM 63
Mesa, Ghost Ranch, NM 64
The Same Mesa, Ghost Ranch, NM 65
Story of Time, Ghost Ranch, NM 66
Nightfall at Ghost Ranch, NM 67
Imperceptibly 68

The Argument 69
Little Stuff 70
A Meadow's Story, Ghost Ranch, NM 71
A Little More Time 72
Before Sandia Mountain, NM 73
Winter Straw 74
Time and Stone, Ghost Ranch, NM................................75
What to Make of a Rainbow? 77
Beholding 78
Reckoning Time, Ghost Ranch, NM 79
Void, Ghost Ranch, NM...80
Redemption from the Earth 81
Mycoplasma Winter 83
Crocus in Winter..84
Survivor's Wound 85
Recognition..87

WORK AND SOCIETY

Blank 93
Refugees 94
Slash and Burn 96
Triumph of Hate 98
Them..99
In the Cross Hairs 100
Without Windows, Without Light 101
Corporate Greed 102
Rules 103
The Box 105
Boxes Everywhere 107
Where is the Blood? 109
Downsizing 111
The Wrong Ending 112
Company Man 113

Keeping the Lawn Trimmed, or How I Became a
    Better Citizen 114
We Have to Leave 116
Psalm Eight, a Revision 117
Just Like TV 119
A Little Morning Music Under Stalin 121
How Things Work Around Here 122
Black Sparks 123
Dermatology 125
Stewardship 126
Welcome 129

PERMISSIONS 131

ON A PERSONAL NOTE 141

ACKNOWLEDGMENTS

In my life as an applied, organizational, psychoanalytic, and medical anthropologist, as well as psychohistorian, and an organizational consultant and poet, many people have opened doors for me. I did not do it all myself! To be "claimed," to be told, in essence, "You and your voice belong here," is one of life's most precious gifts.

Here, I wish to acknowledge the generous encouragement and support of Inna Rozentsvit, M.D., Editor -in-Chief and Publisher of the ORI Academic Press and MindMend Publishing, in helping me to first imagine this book, then to make it into a reality. My thanks go to the gifted artist and poet Sandra Indig, for contributing her paintings for this book.

Over the years, I have been blessed by the encouragement of my poetic efforts by many people: Dr. Seth Allcorn; Dr. Michael Diamond; poet and writer Dolores Brandon; Dr. Molly Castelloe; psychohistorian and poet Dr. Peter Petschauer; Dr. Johanna Shapiro, Poetry Co-Editor of *Pulse – Voices from the Heart of Medicine*; Dr. Susan McDaniel, former Co-Editor of *Families, Systems and Health*; Dr. Warren Holleman, former Poetry Editor of *The Journal of Family Practice*; John Frey, M.D., former editor of *Family Medicine*; Paul Fischer, M.D., former editor of *The Journal of Family Practice*; James Gilbert, M.D.; long-time Enid, Oklahoma, poet Maxine Austin; poet Vivian Stewart; Madelyn Eastlund, long-time Editor of *Harp-Strings Poetry Journal*; Dr. Stephen Stewart, former Editor of *The Applied Anthropologist*; Dr. Paul Elovitz, Editor of *Clio's Psyche*; Dr. Lenora Bohren; Dr. Deward E. Walker, Jr., former editor of *High Plains Applied Anthropologist*; Dr.

Ed Knop; Dr. Jack Schultz; Dr. J. Neil Henderson, long-time Director of the American Indian Diabetes Prevention Center; Nathan Gunter, Managing Editor of *vox poetica* and of *Oklahoma Today Magazine,* and his predecessors at *Oklahoma Today*, Steffie Corcoran, Senior Editor, and earlier, Louisa McCune, Senior Editor; the International Psychohistorical Association; the High Plains Society for Applied Anthropology (of which I am their Poet Laureate); and countless other people with whom I have worked since I began writing poetry in the late 1980's.

FOREWORD

"What is best in music is not to be found in the notes." – Gustav Mahler

MindMend Publishing is pleased to introduce to the world the first book of poetry in our Consilience Series, *Centre and Circumference*, by Dr. Howard Stein. The concept of consilience – the unity of knowledge, which was introduced by biologist Edward Wilson (1998) – with all its 'jumping together' (of the facts from different fields of knowledge) and linking (sciences and humanities) quality, will be felt by everyone who immerses him/herself in this collection of poetry. Dr. Stein unifies the knowledge of humanity, of what makes us human, from three different perspectives: Love and Life, Time and Memories, Work and Society. Hard core math and physics are not the main ingredients here, but human emotions that connect to common sense and intellect, to the universe, and to rhythms of music and poetry, take center stage. As Sigmund Freud once said, 'Poets are masters of us ordinary men, in knowledge of the mind, because they drink at streams which we have not yet made accessible to science.'

Dr. Stein is described by friends and colleagues as a poet, poet laureate; applied / psychoanalytic / organizational / medical anthropologist; psychohistorian; and finally, a Renaissance man. All these descriptions, titles, and nominations offer us an idea about who Howard Stein is: he is someone who engages with human experience in all its complexity and beauty; someone who does not impose his 'rules' and assumptions onto others; someone who can appreciate 'the other' without losing the 'self'; someone who can share, and not only teach; and someone who can listen. Very much like the late Oliver Sacks, Howard Stein offers 'anthropological house calls' (Sacks's term), while the 'house' is not one's apartment, but all humanity's soul.

Howard Stein and Oliver Sacks share many other interests and qualities. One of them is the ability to listen with 'benevolent curiosity' (Freud, 1923), to appreciate people for who they are, and not for what they ought to be; to feel the situation through, with all the filaments of one's soul; to hold off interpretations and let them percolate, as in Bion's (1962) 'container / contained'; and then listen some more, 'without memory and desire' (Bion, 1964). They both provide the subjects of their examination a 'transitional space,' and a place to 'be' and to 'play' (Winnicott, 1951; 1971), and an idea that no matter how hard and impossible life seems to be – it is all worth it! They both turn 'grey theory' about any human situation into 'perpetual green experience' (Freud, 1924). And, although neither Howard Stein nor Oliver Sacks were formally trained in psychoanalysis, they can be considered to be poet laureates of psychoanalytic thought and psychoanalytic technique.

Another quality unites these great men: Stein and Sacks are both gentle and unique storytellers. They tell stories that reflect the reality of life, in a very poetic way, even stories related to medical conditions (read *Mycoplasma Winter* or *Dermatology* here!); stories that one would never want to put out there, as these stories remind us of our mortality, our fragility, our 'neediness' for another, and a not-so-attractive inability to hold it all together at times. There is a great deal of overlap between the neurotic and the aesthetic (Burke, 1939), and Stein's poetry can definitely be used to illustrate this phenomenon. Just listen to this:

FOREWORD

> What is the purpose
> for my heart to beat
> if it's not for you?
> What is the reason
> for my heart to break
> if it's not over you?
> (from Howard Stein's *Purpose*, p. 20)

Both Stein and Sacks appreciate music, on a very intimate and even existential level. They love music, they breathe music, and they think in music terms. As Dr. Stein explained once, when we were discussing the possibility of using some fragments of musical notations in this book, that when he writes, teaches, or engages in conversation, he wonders about 'what piece of music going on' in his head and in his soul.

We never asked Dr. Stein (or simply, Howard) of how he would like to be remembered in 100 years, but Oliver Sacks summed it up for both of them when he responded to this question by saying that he wants people to remember him listening to them 'carefully,' and trying 'to imagine what it was like for them,' and trying to convey this..., and to use a biblical term, the feeling, "he bore witness."' They both bear witness.

So, we hope that you enjoy this collection of poems, and feel through your heart, mind, and soul that very viral, enormous, love that Howard Stein has for people and for the human condition, for music and poetry, and for life. Just do the 'immersion,' and the rest will come, as Dr. Stein would say.

Inna Rozentsvit, Editor, on behalf of
MindMend Publishing & ORI Academic Press

INTRODUCTION

The phrase, "centre and circumference," the title of this poetry collection, comes from Percy Bysshe Shelley's 1821 essay, *A Defence of Poetry.** Shelley's metaphor is how I have come to imagine poetry – in fact all the arts – as well. In his essay, Shelley (1821/1840) writes,

> ... Poetry is at once the centre and circumference of knowledge; it is that which comprehends all science, and that to which all science must be referred. It is at the same time the root and blossom of all other systems of thought; it is that from which all spring, and that which adorns all; and that which, if blighted, denies the fruit and seed, and withholds from the barren world the nourishment and the succession of the scions of the tree of life. ...Poetry enlarges the circumference of the imagination by replenishing it with thoughts of ever new delight, which have the power of attracting and assimilating to their own nature all other thoughts. ...

In a world obsessed with facts (even deceptive "alternate facts"), Albert Einstein insisted that "imagination is more important than knowledge." Many scientists and philosophers, including Arthur Zajonc (2014)**, have likewise restored imagination to its place as the ultimate source of all ways of knowing both self and external world. In the least, there are many ways of knowing. Poetry, far from being an afterthought and poor second to regal science, liberates and revitalizes thought. Far from being diminished by science, poetry can inform and rescue science as well as, in turn, be inspired by science.

Far from representing a forever turning-away, inward, from the world, poetry (nerve endings of which reach both outward and inward in constant dialogue) is an essential instrument for knowing the world. "Subjectivity" is an instrument of greater, not lesser, "objectivity." The poet's unconscious is stimulated by worlds within and beyond, in a kind of eternal dance. Words, as written, read, spoken, and heard, are the fruit of this dance. The poet does not write in a void. All creativity is intersubjective, the fruit of dialogue.

I hope that the poems in this collection enlarge the compass of your imagination, of your world, and of your engagement with it. I have a further wish that dwells in the invisible bond between poet and reader. In the words inscribed by Beethoven on his *Missa Solemnis*, "From the heart, may it go again to the heart" ("*Von Herzen, möge es wieder, zu Herzen gehen!*").

*Shelley, P. B. (1821/1840). *A Defence of Poetry*. Retrieved on April 10, 2018 from http://www.bartleby.com/27/23.html.

**Zajonc, A. (February 7, 2014). "Intention and Imagination in Higher Education," The Center for Contemplative Mind in Society. http://www.contemplativemind.org/archives/2698.

Sandra Indig, *Blue Energy II*,
acrylic on canvas, 23''x19''

LOVE and LIFE

COMPANIONSHIP

Sea gently
laps its shore;
Sea assaults its coast
with merciless abandon.
Two moods –
perfect symmetry.

No sea without its shore,
no shore without its sea –
calm and violence
keep each other
good company.

Sandra Indig, *Blue Line*,
acrylic on canvas, 26''x30''

EMBRACES

You hugging me,
I hugging you –
not so easily parsed
as it may appear.
Your arms envelop
my body, as if
they could reach
all the way around.
I respond in kind,
as if you had extended
an invitation.

Soon I could not tell
where your hug ended
and mine began.
For a moment,
two lives held
by a single embrace,
as if the hug
had an existence
all its own
and we were
but its fulfillment.

UNANSWERED QUESTIONS

Is impossible
ever possible?
Shall I renounce
hope that finding
will ever be matched
by being found?

I wander the earth
seeking you.
If I find you,
will your eyes
turn away from mine,
just when I thought
they had met?
If I find you,
will I be also found?

NOTHING

Your smiling eyes
met mine and stayed,
a kind of skin on skin,
as if eyes could touch.

Perhaps it was nothing
more than a trick
my longing played on me
to turn desire into
a kind of perception.

Beethoven, *Moonlight Sonata*,
fragment of musical notation

Sandra Indig, *Violet Series* (2 of 5), acrylic on canvas, 17''x14''

TWEET AND TEXT

Tell me, my love,
what can you say
on your smart phone
that you can't say to me?
You insist you can't
be connected and still
talk with me.
You'd rather tweet and text
than hold hands
across the kitchen table.
You say your hands
need to be free
to work your handheld.
You type on your smartphone
while your open laptop
sits in your lap
as we watch TV.
How long has it been
since you last let me
cross your borders
and let me into
your electronic space?
I hear the sound
of clicking keys
even in my sleep.

PLANETARY

As a planet
orbits its star,
so do I
orbit you –

your gravity,
my desire;
your desire,
my velocity.

Out of what desire
were sun and planet
spun, long ago
in the spiral arm

of a galaxy
made of mere
dust and love?

ONCE

Missing you is part of
remembering you when
forgetting you is impossible.
Perhaps one day your face will be
an image I once knew in flesh;
a tincture of wistfulness
will take the place of throbbing pain.
Once upon a time
will be enough –
but not yet.

METRIC

I do not know
which brings
the greater grief,
the distance
or the longing.

You are my desire,
and you are
beyond touch.
My heartbeat marks
the halting rhythm
of your absence.

What does it matter
the day of the week,
if I am without you?

By what metric
do you measure
the void that has
taken your place?

CRESCENDO

Desire
I desire
I desire you
You are my desire

Love
I love
I love you
You are my love

Without you
the candle
has no flame.
A perfect ratio
of fuel, heat,
and oxygen
fails to ignite
the solitary wick.
You are the fire
for whom the candle waits.

DISAPPOINTMENT

Did you give me hope,
or did I simply hope too much?
Was *impossible* ever *possible*?
Did I just dream too much?
Finding and being found
are such a happenstance thing,
it's a wonder lovers ever meet.

Sandra Indig, *Camp 9: Cancer and Threads of Hope*
(4 of 6), acrylic on rice paper, 9"x12"

WHAT'S LEFT

of love,
what's left is longing –
for you, with no advance description,
until I recognize you –
of course,
whom I've been seeking
all along.

Sandra Indig, *Parade in Blue*,
acrylic on canvas, 11" x 14"

HANDS

strong hands
warm hands
gentle hands
inviting hands

hands that
fit perfectly
enfolded with mine
your hands

Johannes Brahms, piano pieces,
fragment of musical notation

***LIEBESLIEDER GEDICHTE*,**
LOVE SONG POEMS
    after Johannes Brahms

Where will I find you –
will I ever find you –
are you there to be found?

You, we,
figment of imagination's desire
chimera of hope
bride of despair

Since the time
desire began
I have desired
you

incarcerated
by words
liberated
by silence
redeemed
by touch.

It is good to read
but not too much;
it is good to think
but not too much;
it is good to dream
but not too much.
To love you is good

but never enough

Many women
turn my head.
You're the one
who turns my heart.

The thought of you
improves my
vital signs.

precious jewels
precious metals
precious pearls
you

Sandra Indig, *Women*,
charcoal on paper, 10"x14"

THE REACH

Your fingers reached for my hand.
I felt their approach;
I felt them touch me
before they arrived.
They felt. I felt.
They lingered. I lingered.
On a dare,
I took your fingers
into mine.
You did not retreat –
nor did I.
How wondrous that our fingers
could find each other
and stay a while.

PURPOSE

What is the purpose
for my heart to beat
if it's not for you?
What is the reason
for my heart to break
if it's not over you?

Every Don Quixote
has his Dulcinea
he hopes will appear
to him in the flesh.
And what Dulcinea
does not have her Quixote
who she hopes will quicken
out of thin air?

Who is not made of clichés
waiting for their moment,
and be clichés no more?

*GEMÜTLICH / GEMÜTLICHKEIT**

a constellation
of warm feelings:
cosy (cosiness)
snug (snugness)
comfortable (comfortableness)
genial (geniality)
friendly (friendliness)
pleasant (pleasantness)
you

*Borrowed from German

THE WALL

She was almost erotic
In her prohibitive sternness.
She dressed herself
Like a wrapped mummy,
Covering and recovering
Every imaginable part of herself –
Except her scornful eyes
That held in contempt any woman
Less armored than she.
She taught her daughters
The same protective shield,
Above all, to suspect
Any man's intentions.
Who would know – least of all she –
That behind her impregnable wall
Lay an avalanche of desire
Held back only by her hatred
Of who she might have become?

FILAMENT

The world is held together
Not by glass or steel,
But by the thinnest filament,
Unseen but yet more real.
Its strands can come from anywhere,
Below or from above,
It weaves with great tenacity
And has the name of love.

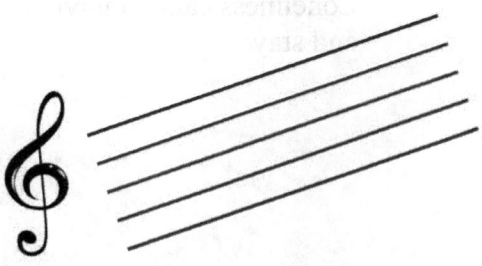

LONELINESS

Loneliness is a person,
a someone, a companion,
a piano sonata with violin *obbligato*,
an absence palpable as a presence,
who travels with me
to every place and occasion.
A desert without oasis,
a prison-cell from which
the key is long ago lost,
a hope devoid of hope,
a future as hypoxic as the present
and the past that birthed it.
Loneliness is the search
for someone who
will neither come nor return.
Loneliness came uninvited –
and stayed.

ICE

Ice – good for inflammation,
good for glaciers,
good for Scotch.

Not good for the heart,
not good for touch.

Fire – melts the heart,
warms the touch,
restores life
from the ice of death.

Sandra Indig, *Fire and Ice*, oil on canvas, 12"x16"

Sandra Indig, *Evocations for Jacques II*, acrylic on canvas, 19"x24"

A SPLASH OF COLD WATER

love's futility
                         acceptance
awaken from my dream
                         our station is to protect
to the barricades
splash cold water on my face
                         go on down the road
run errands
                         hurl myself into work
count serial sevens up to a thousand
listen to *Les Pecheurs de Perles*
                         which brings me back to you
love
    inescapable
        insurmountable
            indelible
                impossible
Magic Fire Music
                         waiting to awaken
from the kiss
                         that never comes
love nonetheless *sotto voce*
a holy quiet covers me with its blanket
I fall asleep with your name
                         on my lips

PRIZE SONG, AFTER WAGNER

I pay my entry fee
for the song contest,
and sing the prize song.
So much is at stake –
to have desire at last
met by desire.
Mine is the wrong song;
I am no *Heldentenor*.
Eva is won by another.
Hope reached out again
into the void.
I cling to my song,
hum it softly to myself,
and walk away,
in meinem Himmel,
in meinem Lieben,
in meinem Lied*

---

*Gustav Mahler, *Rückert Lieder,*
"Ich bin der Welt abhanden gekommen."
Translation from German:
In my Heaven,/In my Love,/in my Song.

ARITHMETIC

Desire entwined
in lovers' bodies,
seeking, reaching,
at last touching,
passion no matter
of simple addition –
one plus one equals two;
but alchemy of yearning,
where two transmutes into one,
swelling in Wagnerian sonorities,
cosmic consummation and release
in soak-filled exhaustion,
then gentle sleep –
until the one awakes
again as two.

CONTRADICTIONS

waiting
hoping
afraid to hope
trying not to hope
unable not to hope
holding my breath
until you appear
unable to hold my breath
that long
not ready to release you
to the winds

FLAW

My worst flaw,
to put words
to glances and gestures –
your lingering pat
on my forearm,
or the gleam in your eye
as we talk.
To name them is taboo,
a secret to be kept
to ourselves,
maybe even from ourselves,
never to be spoken of
between us.

I promise to
keep it to myself –
just don't ask me
to say it didn't happen.

CHARACTER
after J. Neil Henderson

An elderly Choctaw woman,
so much medically wrong with her:
bad heart, bad kidneys, bad brain, swollen legs.
She cusses at her husband, her kids,
her grandkids – anyone is fair game.
Maybe all that's wrong with her
makes her mean, but her family,
church, and town put up with her.

Now and then she'll say she talks
to relatives long dead, to dead horses
and cows, "on the other side," they call it.
She tells folks here what she saw and heard.
Most folks don't say that
it's the disease speaking,
but think she has special powers.
Maybe that's why they put up
with all her fussin'.
Her granddaughter says,
"Maybe she sees things that we don't see,
and communicates in ways we can't" –
which makes her
more a blessing than a curse.

DEFIANCE

Of course, the sun
rises without you.
Do you think
you defy gravity?
That to you, the special theory
of relativity doesn't apply?
Or the second law
of thermodynamics?
You are a most ordinary
datum of physics,
chemistry, and biology.

Your you-ness, though,
defies all your resemblances,
all the laws of nature you obey.
Your gaze outshines
a thousand stars
of first magnitude --
and yes, without you
the sun does not rise.

Sandra Indig, *Black & White Orchids*,
acrylic on canvas, 11''x14''

PACING

I paced the floor
inside my mind,
waiting word
on my son's surgery –
waiting for news,
waiting for results,
waiting for a door
to open,
waiting for someone
to speak with me.

The door stayed shut.

Time stopped.
The room became heavy with
my imagination – unreliable,
my fears – dangerous,
my hopes – unsure.

Waiting grew heavier –
without reprieve,
without resolution,
without grace.

The door stayed shut.

AFTER YOU DIED

Since you died
even fresh coffee tastes bitter.
I recite Hebrew prayers
in your memory,
mutter fragments of *Psalms*
that float across my mind.
My gut tightens into a strangle hold,
as if my colon could
somehow still clutch you.
What irony: my body
tries in vain to do
what my mind cannot.

You are dead – maybe gone over
to some Other Side of the universe,
though "perhaps" is no consolation.
Our familiar melodies enter my mind –
Smetana's *Má Vlast*,
Dvořák's *Slavonic Dances*
and *Eighth Symphony* –
comforting reminders that keep you near.
Since you died even my roses
have turned black with grief.
I have been unable to cry –
fearing to drown in my tears.

Your shadow lengthens
with each passing day.

CONVENTIONS
>for High Plains Society for Applied
>Anthropology, Denver, CO (April),
>Ghost Ranch, NM (September)

In April, September
is not soon enough;
in September, April
is not soon enough.
Two conventions,
two airplanes
to and from.

Three days each
of muted ecstasy,
seeing you once again,
time for what we call
visiting and catching up,
eyes locked in embrace,
like a telescope honed to its star.
The unsaid more palpable
than the spoken,
inducing in me
a sharp pang of arrhythmia.

At meeting's end,
we return to our lives.
At parting, our hugs linger.
We bid each other
to take good care of yourselves.
Then the longing sets in –
until April..., until September....

THE CELLIST
        to the memory of Gregor Piatigorsky

He pulls off
Brahms, Dvořák, Elgar, and Shostakovich
with panache;

He sways
with his instrument
like a ballroom dancer with a perfect partner;

He grimaces
with utmost conviction
as he negotiates strenuous passages;

He feigns
ecstasy with cultivated
lack of affectation;

He plays
with burnished sheen
and resplendent flair;

He is a celebrity;
he looks good.

Sandra Indig, *Confrontation with Mortality*, acrylic on canvas, 19" x 19"

TIME and MEMORIES

VISIT TO A CLOCK REPAIR SHOP

I open the shop door –
clocks everywhere:
big clocks, little clocks,
floor clocks, table clocks,
one clock frozen in time,
another caught speeding.
Clang! Gong! Chime! they sound,
unsynchronized at their quarter hour.

A new customer, clock in hand,
I stand dazzled before
the clatter
of sights and sounds.
For a moment, I forget
why I came.

KEYS

Keys in dishes
Keys in drawers
Keys in ash trays
Keys in jars

Keys that once
Locked and unlocked
Places I knew well –
A set of car keys
Forty-five years old,
But mostly no longer connection
Between key and place.
No link between
Signifier and signified.

There is no more unlocking
With these keys.
The keys themselves
Are now forever locked.
They hold secrets
They cannot tell.
Strange to think metal
Could float in time
Like characters adrift
In Chagall paintings.

I cannot throw
My keys away.
Strewn, yet locked,
They are my life.

PALPABLE

a new book of mine soon to be published
I can hardly wait to hold it in my hands
for a moment forget the words it contains
most important its touch to hungry fingers
materialize into something palpable
no longer just in the mind just in hope

a book is not skin
not body not touch in return
who can hug a book
and be hugged back
or make love with pages
of hard-bound paper
consolation then
at least my longing fingers
can run over the surface
of a book my book

touch and its absence
mostly absence
even when the book
finally arrives

AT THE ART EXHIBIT

An Edward Hopper exhibit
came to town.
I stroll the gallery,
stare at each painting
as if it were familiar.
My eyes walk me into
painting after painting
until they become alive.
I live here; I have lived here
for as long as I can remember –
barren walls, chairs all pointed
away from each other,
afternoon shadows
fallen on unused furniture,
mute red brick buildings
through the window.
No sign of life here.
I disappear into the paintings,
never to return.

DEDICATION

They stood upon my mother's grave,
one, my family's rabbi, a *Litvak*,*
the other, my family's doctor, a Romanian.
Both, Jews -- the rabbi,
heir to generations of Talmudic scholars,
the physician, descendant of the Jewish
outcast *Schwartze Yidn*,**
by legend illiterate and uncouth.
Despite his renown, my doctor
yielded ground to my rabbi,
who had the last word
and the highest place.
My father and I watched
with amusement this little drama,
where Europe trumped America,
rabbi trumped physician,
and everyone else trumped Romania.
The ladder of merit affirmed,
we could get on with what
we had gathered for here in the first place:
prayers to Heaven to unveil
my mother's gravestone.

I will always remember the day
Heaven exalted earth,
and G-d had to wait his turn.

* Lithuanian Jews
** "Black Jews" (pejorative);
my father was also a Romanian Jew

Sandra Indig, *Movable Feast* (diptych, left panel)
acrylic on canvas, 38''x49''

UNCLE HYMEN*
In memoriam

Dear Uncle Hymen,

You died a year before I was born,
yet have pursued me all my life.
You were killed while attacking
a German bunker in the Ardennes,
the Battle of the Bulge.

You were wounded twice before.
While still recovering, you
went back to be with your men.
In my attic the I found a box
containing your medals
and the flag of your burial.

My father named me for you
and often called me by your name.
Sometimes I thought we both
should have been buried
in that cemetery in Luxembourg,
for I could never live up
to your valor and sacrifice.

If I am you, what am I called upon
to do to end the grief that has been
my companion all these years?
Is it my duty to keep your memory alive,
or to allow you finally to have died?

Once I have had your flag repaired

and cleaned, may I drape it over
the coffin in my mind, and allow
both of us, at last, to be at rest?

Your grateful nephew,

*1st Sgt. HYMEN H. STEIN
2nd Infantry, 5th Division, U.S. Army
KILLED IN ACTION
World War II, Ardennes Offensive,
19 January 1945

Shostakovich, *Symphony 5*,
fragment of musical notation

PRESSED LEAF

On page two hundred eighty-six,
to be precise, I ran across
a once-yellow cottonwood leaf
I had planted in the book
long ago. I have many leaves
tucked away in many books.
Well-preserved, still, this one was
imperfect in shape
and unremarkable in residual color.
I could no longer remember
why, of all leaves, I had bent down
and chosen this one to keep.
I felt comforted, though, as if
I had met an old friend.
There was nothing special
about this leaf – except, perhaps,
that it was mine, and had been so
for a very long time.

MESAS AND MEADOWS, GHOST RANCH, NM

Two hundred million years
pass in a fleeting second —
one moment, dinosaurs roam
equatorial marshlands;
in the next, high desert meadows
carpet the valley
with hay fields, cattle,
and tall stalks of yellow chamisa.
What is this mind
that can travel faster
than the speed of light,
and discern time
in a glance at tall strata
of ancient mesas?
I do not know which
is the greater marvel,
the rapid change of hues
in the setting sun—
or the ability
to notice it at all.

SOVEREIGNTY IN THE MESAS, GHOST RANCH, NM

The lord of the mesa reigns*
The lord of the mesa remembers*
The lord of the mesa reveals*

Metaphors of sovereignty
dwell in mesas like spirits,
emanate from mute stone –
tell of sandstone's long dynasty,
dominion's ruddy glow
at sunrise and sunset.
Enthroned in majesty,
mesas crown the long valley
beneath their steep faces –
time's serene nobility
embedded in rock.

*Adapted from the tri-partite Hebrew liturgy for Rosh Hashanah, *Malchuyoth, Zichronoth, and Shofaroth.*

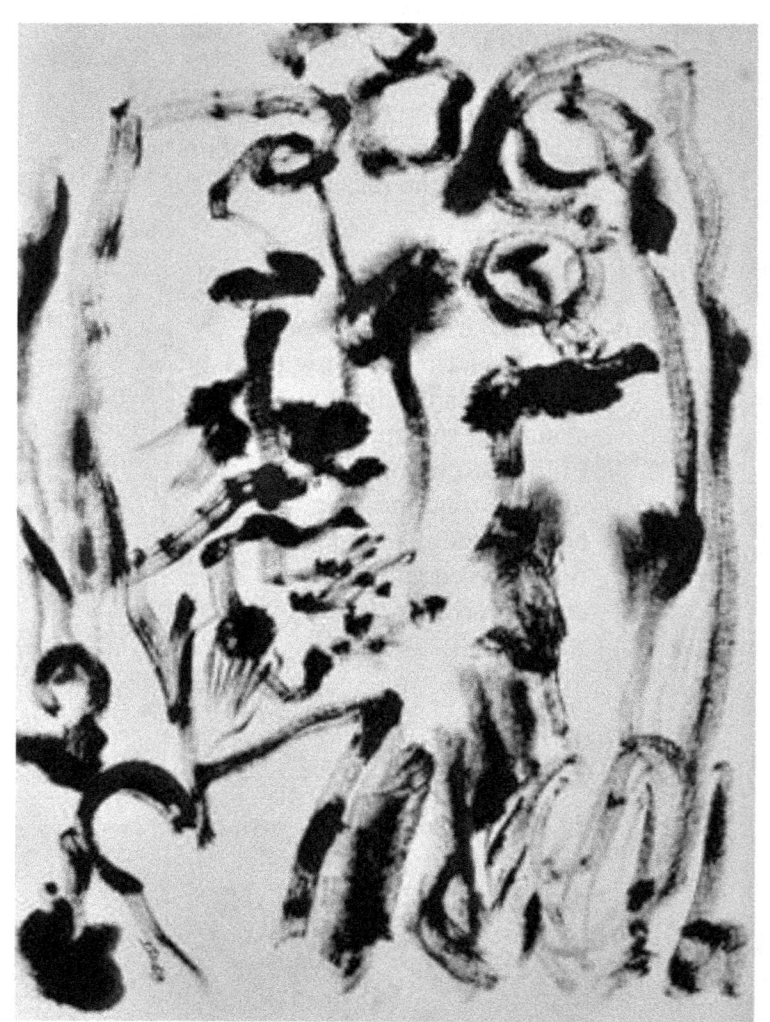

Sandra Indig, *Wall of Prayer*, acrylic on canvas, 36''x24''

INANIMATE, BUT NOT DEAD, GHOST RANCH, NM

Inanimate mesas,
buttes, and spires,
stories and storytellers
in stone –
lack lungs, larynx,
vocal cords, tongue, and mouth,
but still give voice
to mute rock formations.
This is the epic
Homer would have told if he
had been made of sandstone,
siltstone, mudstone, quartz,
and cooled lava flow.
Sagas of life
sealed in the silent rock
of ruddy escarpments
that glow at sunset.
Inanimate rocks
are not dead;
they never cease
to tell their stories.
Listen now –
they are speaking.

BRISTLECONE PINE, GREAT BASIN

Silent triumph,
sustained by harshness,
attuned to desolation,
perfect fit
of gnarled arms,
shallow roots,
high desert's killing sun,
deep winter,
and precious little rain.
The bristlecone pine
refuses to die.

Sandra Indig, *Movable Feast* (diptych, right panel),
acrylic on canvas, 38''x49''

LEAVING GHOST RANCH, NM

Faces and folds of steep mesas
nourish my hunger for perspective.
I stand in awe of you,
spirit in stone.
I cannot stay forever
and sate my soul's craving.
I leave you for another year,
perhaps forever.
How to turn presence
into memory?
Driving out the exit
that was only recently entrance,
I look back one last time,
then hope for the solace
of remembering,
this emptiness a kind
of fulfillment.

HIGH DESERT VALLEY, GHOST RANCH, NM

The long valley is inexhaustible;
no set of eyes can possess it –
tens of thousands of acres
of high desert grass and chamisa
nested between mesas and far mountains.
I stand transfixed
by a place more vast
than my expansive ego.

The land conquers me;
I surrender to the long valley
without resistance.
It stakes its claim
upon my willing soul.
I am gratefully possessed.

Tchaikovsky, *May Nights*,
fragment of musical notation

MESAS AND MOUNTAINS, GHOST RANCH, NM

Steep mesas and wide mountains
reckon time in measures
my rushed days cannot fathom.
Geologic clichés,
redeemed by awe,
temper claims of
triumph's duration –
all vanity
faces extinction.
In mesas and mountains
I did not find eternity,
but what I found
was time enough.

Tchaikovsky, *May Nights*,
fragment of musical notation

IT GOES EITHER WAY

Mid fall,
dry leaves cover the ground;
you are
nowhere to be found,
but in the garden,
red roses still bloom.

Mid fall,
dry leaves cover the ground;
in the garden,
red roses still bloom,
but you are
nowhere to be found.

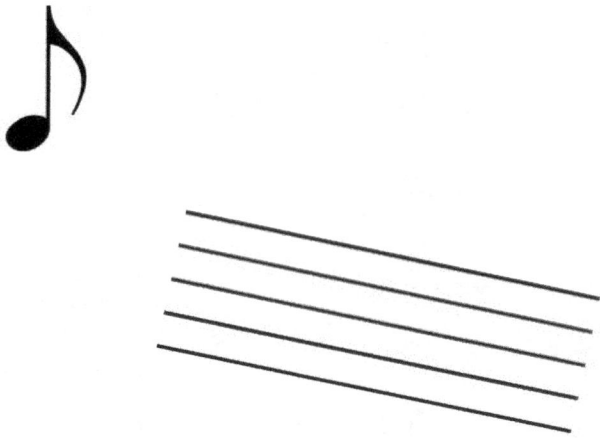

SEEING TWICE

I follow the seasons
as earth encircles sun.
Snow, blossoms,
rich, green leaves,
later red and gold,
bare branches –
nourishment for my eyes,
for my soul,
for the alchemist
of memory.

I sit on my porch
among Oklahoma scrub oak,
rehearse the seasons,

remembering,
with eyes closed.
How fortunate I am
to have the seasons twice –
seasons in Nature,
seasons in mind –
Nature's eyes to see itself.

INVITATION TO THE DANCE
after Carl Maria von Weber

Dry leaves, partner
with wind,
swirl, twirl, skip, scrape
in their dance
to an orchestra
conducted by wind –
dance in the open,
dance in corners
where curbs and walls meet.
Leaves' invisible partner
leads in gusts, in eddies,
in gentle breezes
across the ballroom floor,
till wind tires
and leaves settle down –
awaiting a new partner
to sweep them off their feet.

FILLING IN, GHOST RANCH, NM

In the high New Mexico desert
stand plateaux, buttes, and pinnacles;
between them,
vast canyons and valleys –
all that remain of what were once
thick layers of stone,
and at their base, an inland sea.
Erosion is time's final judgment
upon the upward thrust
of invisible plates.
Even mountains are mortal.

I view this void from the long valley below;
I can almost feel the slow, indomitable
attrition of stone by ice, snow, rain, and wind.
As if by magic, my eyes fill in
what history has erased.
If only for a moment, I reverse time.

MESA, GHOST RANCH, NM

Every mesa has its talus –
Rubble at the foot of majesty.
Sandstone cliffs that tell of time
Yield to time.

What would I think of
A mesa without its shards?
Do they not both glow
At sunset?

I scaled the mesa's face
With my eyes –
They told me
Prominence and heap are one.

THE SAME MESA, GHOST RANCH, NM

I stand in the grassy lowland,
my gaze fixed upon
the face of the vast cliff before me.

Over many days, over many years,
the face of the mesa
displays many moods, many temperaments,
shaped by the angle of the sun,
the clouds that shade it,
rain, snow, wind, and ice,
even the place where I stand,
transfixed.

The same mesa is never
the same mesa next time –
but an inexhaustible place,
an inexhaustible face,
drawing me near
to introduce itself.
I return to stand in its mute presence –
and feel renewed by this ancient stone.

STORY OF TIME, GHOST RANCH, NM

Ancient buttes and mesas
tell the story of time,
of muscular buildups
and staccato breakdowns,
ages that measure our lives
by the history of the earth –
fathomless time,
exalted time,
time beyond time
in a story told by stone.

Sandra Indig, *Reflections in Plastic - Darker Side*,
acrylic on canvas, 8''x11''

NIGHTFALL AT GHOST RANCH, NM

Shadows deepen in the mesas' folds,
lengthen east of a row of cottonwood.
The Pedernal* and companion mountains
turn ash gray at dusk.
Time for night to settle.
Darkness is not permanent.
The Pedernal will be among the first
to greet the sun.

*The Cerro Pedernal is a flat-topped extinct volcano south of Ghost Ranch, Abiquiu, NM. It was made famous by artist Georgia O'Keefe's numerous paintings and sketches.

IMPERCEPTIBLY

Imperceptibly,
The space between branches grows.
Autumn flirts with sky.
Cottonwood leaves turn pastel yellow;
Scrub oak leaves turn mostly brown.

I do not know what I wish more –
For the leaves to linger or to fall,
How much of the night I want to see.
Autumn does not ask my preference;
It slowly does its work
Through the chill, the wind, and the rain.

Imperceptibly,
Fall loosens the bond of summer
And prepares me for winter
And a vaster sky.

Tchaikovsky, *Seasons: Autumn Song,*
fragment of musical notation

THE ARGUMENT

Winter picked an argument
with reluctant fall,
who responded in kind
with a burst of dazzling color.
But autumn proved no match
for cold wind and intrepid rain,
until they raked most leaves
from their branches
and hurled them to the ground.
Early winter made a rich lawn,
crisp to trample on,
then brought in snow and ice
to seal the dispute.
Winter clinched the argument
hands down.

Tchaikovsky, *Winter Dreams,*
fragment of musical notation

LITTLE STUFF

A lush meadow on a country drive.
Deep green after a spring rain;
broad oak leaves,
opened like a hand,
after the long crypt of winter;
a pastel blue sky
and a gentle breeze –
hardly worthy
of the ten o'clock news –
greeting card clichés.
Little stuff, maybe,
but nourishment
for my reverie.

A MEADOW'S STORY, GHOST RANCH, NM

A long meadow
stretches to the far mountains
that act as a rim to the Chama Valley,
eons ago an inland sea.
Dinosaurs called the place home.

Today, we tremble at the thought
of our own extinction,
caused not by an asteroid,
but by ourselves.

Sandra Indig, *Innisfree*,
lithograph on archival paper, 13" x 19"

A LITTLE MORE TIME

Autumn leans into winter,
as cold wind and rain strip most leaves
from their summer moorings.
A small corner of the yard, though,
fails to listen to reason. There,
rosebushes bloom once more,
as if nature could defy nature
one last time before frost,
deny winter's harsh decree
another day, another week –
until even stubborn beauty
can no longer fend off winter,
and surrenders its tender petals
to the tilt of the earth
away from the sun.

BEFORE SANDIA MOUNTAIN, NEW MEXICO
for Ed Knop

Mysterious mountain,
sacred to Pueblo tribes,
towers above the desert.
Forested on the east side,
its sheer drop on the west side
glows iridescent red
when the sun sinks low.
It draws me near
as I pass it by.
An ancient aura surrounds it –
there is power in this place.
Its power flows
to anyone who will receive it.

WINTER STRAW

Brittle straw, immense fields
of scruffy grass
faded flaxen from winter's bite,
once rich green from spring,
parched brown from summer,
a hint of rust in fall.
Then enter winter,
color's final thief.
The llano's stiff straw awaits
its winter coating:
a glaze of ice,
a sea of snow.
Cows revel in bales
of alfalfa hay when snow
buries buffalo grass too far below.
If winter is to rest,
it is more so to endure.
Spring is not yet probable –
let alone inevitable.

TIME AND STONE, GHOST RANCH, NM

Canyons and mesas,
mountains and valleys,
steep cliffs and detritus –
silent rocks tell stories
of hundreds of millions of years,
the secret of time in stone.

Awe brings me here
year after year,
to stir my imagination,
to uncover with reverence
the footprint of time.

"I am part of this," I tell myself,
"and all this is part of me."
I give myself over
to my geology,
and offer thanks to be able
to fathom this at all.

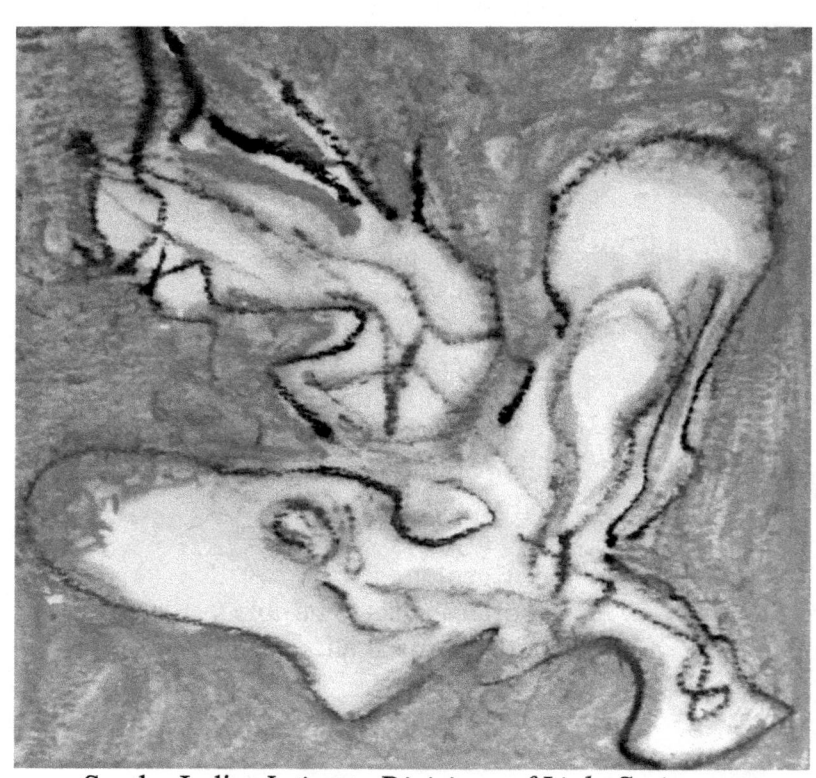

Sandra Indig, *Intimate Divisions of Light Series*, Part 4:3, watercolor on paper, 8"x8"

WHAT TO MAKE OF A RAINBOW?
to the memory of Olivier Messiaen

Years ago,
after a summer storm,
a rainbow arced
across the prairie sky,
took me by surprise.

I asked for no gold
where it touched land,
only company and comfort
in a menacing sky.
I offered, in return,
gratitude and awe.

Over decades of insult,
Jew-baiting, and humiliation
where I worked,
it appeared like a gift,
from where I do not know.

Do I read into Nature,
or does Nature
read into me?

I do not look for signs,
yet my rainbow abides,
answer to a question
I had not thought to ask.

BEHOLDING

Majestic as the crowns
of the Hapsburgs, the Hohenzollerns,
and the Romanovs;
splendid as the vaulted ceilings
of medieval cathedrals;
leaves on arching branches
of scrub oak
glow translucent gold
toward sunset in mid-autumn.
For a moment, the gleaming roof
seems to hover.

To think I could have missed this all
had I not leaned backwards
as far as I could,
and looked straight up
to discover this miracle
of transience and light.

RECKONING TIME, GHOST RANCH, NM

Everything
here sprawls –
mesas, buttes, desert valleys,
cottonwood roots, sky;
They tell the same story
of reckoning time:
luminescent canyons
that glow in a low sun;
high desert
that was once a sea.
In this place
intrepid life grows
where it can
and asks for little
in return.
Space is parable,
mask of sprawling time.

VOID,
GHOST RANCH, NM

A deep, wide canyon stretches
between tall mesas and mountains;

    in its space sky begins;
    sometimes, it bestows comforting stillness;
    other times, fierce storms
    assault the valley without warning.

Imagination fills in
what erosion took away.
Sandstone buttes and spires
preserve geology's memory.

    This place is not empty –
    in its basin time dwells
    and never leaves.

REDEMPTION FROM THE EARTH

I have tasted
contempt for the earth.
It is bitter – better to wager
on incorporeal afterlife
after we have wasted our home.
The body we inhabit
already decomposes;
our open sores reek
of our self-inflicted wounds.

Nowhere to hide –
no Rome, no Jerusalem,
no Mecca, no petroglyphs,
no holy places will be left.
Wastewater oceans,
putrefied skies.
We have taken our poison
and await its effects.
No one will be left
to mourn us
and the pearl that gave us life.

We don't need G-d
to send us plagues.
We are the Angel of Death
we have sent to dwell among us
and bring us to ruin.
No blood on the doorpost
will save us now.

Sandra Indig, *Yellow Sphere #2*,
acrylic on canvas, 7.5"x9.5"

MYCOPLASMA WINTER

It was a mycoplasma winter,
atypical pneumonia,
without a cell wall,
able to survive without oxygen –
without mercy for its host.
This mycoplasma
joined forces with asthma,
each breath now a triumph.

The same two months,
waves of ice and snow
suffocated the ground.
Who dared walk or drive far
in such an unyielding arctic clutch?
When the calendar finally said spring,
winter took exception,
did not lift its siege –

and lingered unwelcomed,
like the mycoplasma that,
spiteful of all medicine,
stayed as if it owned the place.
It came to feast
and not to spare.

CROCUS IN WINTER

A crocus poked its head
through late winter snow,
heedless of timing
in an engulfing sea.

Why I turned my head
toward it,
I'll never know –
perhaps I was ready to behold.

Sandra Indig, *Collage on Black*, aquarelle, 10"x13"

SURVIVOR'S WOUND
In memoriam, Paul Celan

If none will see
    Atrocity,
Does the survivor
    Have a wound?

If I screamed and no one
    Heard me,
Would I have screamed
    At all?

My torment is double:
    Holes in my flesh
    And holes in time.

I speak for the dying
    And for the dead:
Affirm, at least,
    My scream!

Nothing happened,
You whisper back –
    Nothing;
Your atrocity is
    But a dream.

If none will see
    Atrocity,
Does the survivor
    Have a wound?

Sandra Indig, *Rolled into Tilson*,
acrylic on board, 9"x12"

RECOGNITION
for H. B.

For the longest time,
there seemed to be two of you;
I realized at last there is one.

I think I finally recognize you,
my doctor friend –
You give me extra time
when I come to see you;
you fight with insurance companies
to pay for my treatment;
you are always at the legislature
to demand help for
patients whose sickness
and madness fall through the cracks.
You do not give up.

I connected the missing dots,
my doctor friend –
Your folks fought in the Resistance
(was it Lodz, or was it Warsaw?),
their home, sewers and tunnels
beneath formidable foes.
There was no question
who was more determined,
where resistance itself was victory.

They did not give up then;
nor do you now.
I am grateful for both.

Sandra Indig, *Syblils*,
acrylic on archival paper, 24"x19"

WORK and SOCIETY

BLANK
for Richard Koenigsberg

A blank page,
a blank stare,
pencil going nowhere,
held idly in the hand,
first poised, then limp,
now twitching with anticipation
of words that never come.
Absence, leaden absence,
void with the weight of a black star,
irredeemable time –
a writer's curse and shame.

Then, out of the darkness,
unbeckoned, a strange calm,
a comforting stillness approaches,
emptiness no longer absence,
but now fulfillment,
a quilt of goose down,
this visitor, this companion,
this solitude.

No need for words;
they will come later.

REFUGEES

"Teeming shores,"
"wretched refuse,"
people in vast waves of flight.
They flee, they walk, they run,
they spill over edges of boats,
they float, they swim, they drown,
they seek refuge from endless hate and war,
many unwanted, many welcomed.

Who would have known
twelve years ago
lust for oil and obsession
with unseating a dictator
would lead to this,
worse fanaticism than before?
Rape, bloodshed, and destruction
on an unimaginable scale.
Après nous, le déluge,
the leaders seemed to say –
collateral damage.
In their single-minded ambition,
unintended consequences
do not matter.
Where have all the flower petals gone?

For those in flight, anything is
better than the life from which they run.
Then, the wager that
somewhere, by someone,
a door, a gate, would open;

they would be let in,
and months of flight
would finally end.
There would be the possibility
of settling into home again –
for most, still a dream.

Sandra Indig, *Jacob's Blessing B&W*,
acrylic on vellum, 8.5"x11"

SLASH AND BURN*

O dark, dark, dark, amid the blaze of noon,
Irrecoverably dark, total eclipse
Without all hope of day!
(John Milton, 1671, *Samson Agonistes*)

>Nightfall, then midnight,
>endless night,
>no hope of dawn.
>None can see in this
>piercing darkness.
>
>New words, new phrases,
>impose new reality:
>cloudless sky is downpour,
>falsehood is truth,
>disagreement is betrayal.
>
>Open doors slam shut,
>frantic refugees turned away
>not far from Lady Liberty's beckon;
>the new president promises new walls
>to shut out more escaping aliens.
>
>Whispers – dubious election,
>more like a coup.
>I choke on my words;
>nothing can come out
>except voiceless dread.
>
>Night engulfs all light;

nothing escapes its maw.
Fear victorious,
death triumphant,
Furies rule the night.

*Written the thirteenth day of the Donald Trump's Presidency of the United States, February 1st, 2017.

Mussorgsky, *Boris Godunov*, fragment of musical notation

TRIUMPH OF HATE

"Things fall apart; the centre cannot hold."
(W. B. Yeats, 1919, *The Second Coming*)

    Hate has set love
    to flight and hiding;
    arms of affection,
    too frightened
    to reach out
    toward vulnerable embrace,
    shrivel inward.
    Plains Indians staged raids
    with bows and arrows;
    we point our automatic guns
    toward random human targets,
    mow them down
    by the dozens and more,
    no end to the escalation
    of terror and blood --
    pitiless slaughter
    to avenge new
    and long ago hurts.
    Hate marches smartly
    in endless perfect columns,
    toward fields of engagement,
    where death mounts its
    final campaign over life.
    We are the Beast
    who slouches toward extinction.

THEM

I am a "them" to you –
the banishment is
in your eyes,
in the distance
you stand from me,
in the frown
on your face
when I am the object
of your gaze.
How not to make
your judgment
my own,
and become a "them"
to me?

IN THE CROSS HAIRS

"O mia patria, sì bella e perduta"
(Giuseppe Verdi, 1841, *Nabucco*)

O, my country, to what good end
do you put your people
in the cross hairs of a rifle sight?
What do you so fear that you
spew hate to fend it off?
Were we not all somewhere unwanted,
kept on the other side
of a fiercely guarded wall?
Do we not all fear that which
we so long toiled to attain
will be taken away?
We are all haunted
by the same dark night.
I can see my own reflection
in the face of the foe I would kill.

Come! Let us sit at the same table
and dip our ladle from the same pot.
The vineyards are plentiful;
no one need thirst here.
Let us lower our shields
and put to our lips
a draught of reconciliation.

WITHOUT WINDOWS, WITHOUT LIGHT

This place is without windows,
Without outside light,
Without outside air.
The seasons are changing,
But we would not know.

We work at our stations.
We imagine autumn.
We wear all varieties
Of religious amulets
To simulate the sun.

This place is all brick,
Dark glass, and metal.
It does not have windows;
It does not need windows.
There is nothing to see.

CORPORATE GREED

The corporation has a body,
a hungry body.
The corporation has a mouth,
a chief executive mouth,
and not far below it
a hungry maw,
incapable of being filled.

The chief executive mouth
is urged on toward
greater consumption
by the many other
parts of the body –
accountants and bankers,
attorneys and consultants,
directors and securities dealers,
regulators and financial analysts,
and shareholders.

The chief executive mouth
feeds the corporation,
until at last the corporation,
wasted away,
still empty,
has consumed itself.

RULES

For the newcomer to this workplace,
there are rules to learn:
explicit rules,
unstated rules,
conscious rules,
unconscious rules,
official rules,
informal rules,
rules that are spoken,
rules that are undiscussable,
rules that make sense,
rules that make no sense
but are supposed to make sense.

Your main job is to obey them all,
and you thought you only
came here to work!

Sandra Indig, *Hourglass*, acrylic on canvas, 12''x13''

THE BOX

without warning the security guard
appeared in his office
handed him an empty *box*
ordered him to put
all his personal belongings in it
and accompany the guard
to an auditorium for special processing
he was dazed but followed the command
after all the guard carried a gun
he quickly gathered his things in the *box*
and followed the guard
into the auditorium with many others
the guard locked the door behind him
the CEO entered and announced
that the company had a financial crisis
and had to downsize five thousand
employees immediately
the guard returned and ordered him
to bring his *box* to a long queue with everyone else
turn in his keys and badge and parking card
and everything else that belonged to the company
he brought his *box* clung to it
the guard escorted him to the parking lot
and to his car told him that he would
receive his final paycheck in the mail
in a couple of weeks and that he was
to leave and not return to the company
he held his *box* all the more tightly
sat in his car with his *box* in his lap
for several minutes before

starting the engine drove all over town
with his *box* all that remained
of his twenty-five years with the company
once he arrived home he sat in his
car with his *box* in his hands
he did not get out of his car
for a very long time unsure
whether he was alive or dead
he felt unreal alone with his *box*
the only thing in his life
that felt real now
a coffin of sorts
what would his wife and children say
what would they think of the *box*

Sandra Indig, *Double-Cross-Sticks*,
acrylic on canvas, 9"x12"

BOXES EVERYWHERE

Boxes ubiquitous –
little boxes, big boxes,
enormous boxes,
boxes made of cardboard,
shipping and receiving,
sealing and ripping open,
to be carried out of the building
with personal belongings
when you are fired;
cubicles to work in,
if you manage to keep your job;
office buildings shaped like
giant rectangular boxes;
"little boxes made of ticky tacky"*
out in the suburbs;
surrounded by boxes,
buried in boxes.
Last night, deep in sleep,
I dreamt I had become a box;
when I awoke, it was true.

*from Malvina Reynolds, 1962/ 1990,
Little Boxes

Sandra Indig, *Surprise*,
acrylic on archival paper, 14"x17"

WHERE IS THE BLOOD?

Night at corporate headquarters –
The four of us who studied the company's downsizing
Walk silently through a long, dim-lit,
Blank, cream-painted corridor,
A place where phantoms dwell and wait,
A place where walls seem to close in on us.
We all look around,
As if we are looking for something.
After about twenty paces into this antiseptic cave,
I ask aloud, "Where is the blood?" –
My three friends say they were thinking
The same thing.

A consultant team, all in black suits,
Had recently studied the financial books
And recommended to the CEO
That they could save lots of money
And make the company look good to shareholders
By firing a thousand employees immediately – for starters.
"Mandatory downsizing to keep the company alive,"
"A necessary sacrifice for the sake of the company,"
The leader said to those gathered
In a locked auditorium before they were ordered to stand
In long queues of people processed
Impersonally, efficiently, in a well-oiled machine,
And finally escorted to the parking lot, never to return.

The four of us knew the story,
See it unfold before us again
In that cavern, as we walk and relive it.

The walls and carpet bleed,
Cover our shoes and clothes
In still-warm, thick, crimson blood,
Like in a horror movie.
The story hovers in the air;
Its ghost will not leave.
It speaks to us with great sadness;
Even the ghost could not rid itself of the memory,
Could not abandon the prison of knowing too much.
The four of us look at each other,
The story alive in all of us.

Bathed in fresh blood, we leave the building
And re-enter the night,
Carrying the hall's darkness with us.
We had been through the mass firing
Even before it happened.
We knew too much –
The blood will not wash off,
Not now, maybe never.

DOWNSIZING

What is happening
has not happened,
and if it has,
we do not want to know.

People I worked with yesterday,
today are suddenly whisked away;
no one asks where they go –
or even really wants to know.

There is no blood to show
for all their disappearance;
they just are
not around anymore.

The signs all
read the same –
on the highways, in the stores,
on the elevators, in the halls:

What is happening
has not happened,
and if it has,
we do not want to know.

THE WRONG ENDING

Rubbish is what he felt like –
garbage wrapped in newspaper
and taken out to the metal cans
near the mail box.
After thirty years of service
fired without notice,
a company man his company disowned.
("Where did I go wrong?" he wondered.)
"Dead wood," "trim the fat,"
that's what the paper
said the next morning,
just one of three thousand let go,
all in the same day.
Thrown into the street –
garbage!

COMPANY MAN

Fired ten thousand employees in the US,
hired five thousand people overseas,
away from family three weeks a month,
trained new workers to do the job of two
for less pay than one.

Received promotions and bonuses,
a successful man, a corporate hero,
looked forward to retirement
and time with his family.

Let go without warning
in his thirtieth year
for someone half his age
who could do the job of two
for the price of one.

They told him:
nothing personal, just business,
collateral damage.

No gratitude,
forgotten,
a nobody –
as if he'd never been there.

KEEPING THE LAWN TRIMMED,
OR HOW I BECAME A BETTER CITIZEN

    The rule is only stated
    When it is egregiously violated –
    As when recently an ad hoc
    Committee from my neighborhood
    Arrived at my front door
    At precisely high noon,
    Were as polite as one could ever ask,
    But then pointed out to me –
    As if I could not see for myself –
    That the grass on my lawn
    Was tall and patchy, a sight
    Unseemly to those more
    Used to unbroken, meticulous
    Carpeting in yard upon yard.

    They had kept close tab
    On one another over the years;
    Their lawns luxuriated in thick
    Bermuda grass and fescue,
    Inviting the passer-by for a nap.
    I was new to the area,
    One not much for doting
    On grass and yard.
    I was satisfied so long
    As the snakes and mice kept away.

    But not the committee
    At my front door.
    "Appearance is everything,"

They instructed: "Your yard,"
They continued, "Is a reflection
Of who you are."
Clearly I was out of line,
And did not reflect well on them.
Singlehandedly, I had made
The neighborhood look run down.
Though I protested their priorities,
I capitulated with a vow to become
More neighborly, more like them,
Everything in its place.

Come to think of it,
I could even begin to hear
Patrick Henry of old
Let out with his fiery
Call for freedom:
"I know not what course
Others may take, but as for me,
Give me fescue or give me death."

I knew immediately
What I must do to fulfill
My patriotic duty.

WE HAVE TO LEAVE

We knew our group would end soon –
it said so in the printed conference program.
We had completed our meeting's agenda.
No one moved, but instead continued sitting,
and launched into a new round of ideas,
future conferences, possible themes
for next year and beyond.
If we talked enough about the future,
maybe the sting of parting
could be soothed.
Maybe we wouldn't have to leave –
I wondered.

I broke the spell, said
I had to check out of my hotel
and get to the airport.
As if obeying a signal,
everyone stood up and began
their good-byes, embraced
each other with lingering hugs
that would have to last
in memory until the next time –
both a certainty and a question mark.

PSALM EIGHT, A REVISION

"How glorious is Thy name in all the earth."
(Psalm 8:1)

How glorious is our name in all the earth!
Does not our glory reach above the heavens?
Have we not conquered the depth of the seas?
Does not all the land prostrate itself at our feet?
Who can say to us: "What is it that you do?"
(As if anyone could stop us from doing it)?
Imagination is destiny: We do what we will.
What we think we then make real.
Ours is the dominion of angels and gods;
We have crowned ourselves with glory and honor.
Who is like unto us? We bow to no others.
See how deeply the earth bows to us?
Like a good mother, the earth will make good
Whatever we destroy. We have no limits.
How glorious is our name in all the earth!

Sandra Indig, *Fellowship*,
acrylic on archival paper, 20"x26"

JUST LIKE TV

It's as if they knew the script...

At the café
the men's breakfast group talked about –
the city's latest murder,
the football game's best plays,
the bad storm approaching us
from the northwest.

Then there was the conversation
of folks while they were pumping gasoline –
the terrible robbery downtown at the bank this morning,
the hometown basketball team's miraculous
come-from-behind at yesterday's high school game,
the unseasonably warm weather for January.

Just about everywhere, the same chant –
the grocery store queue at the cash register,
lingering visits at the barber shop,
earnest discussions while drinking beer after work –
everyone knew their lines.

News
Sports
Weather –
life, just like TV.

Shostakovich, *Symphony #7 "Leningrad,"* fragment of musical notation

A LITTLE MORNING MUSIC
UNDER STALIN
for Peter Petschauer

Shostakovich over breakfast
Is not such a good idea –
Not good for the appetite,
Not to mention swallowing
And digestion. Shostakovich
Can be upsetting with his
Infectious tunes followed
By screeching dissonance
And loud hammering,
Eventually ending in crashing bombast
Or exhausted resignation.
His music is an astringent
For the soul, takes you
To places of sorrow and despair
Deeper than Dante's final circle.
Not good at breakfast,
Or any meal, for that matter.
Come to think of it,
There is no good time
For this Russian. His is the land of
Loud knocks on the door
At three in the morning,
And disappearance to the vanishing point.
Listen to Shostakovich only
When you have the stomach
For a world you could not make up.

HOW THINGS WORK AROUND HERE

Dear Mr. Stein:
This is the Department of
How Things Work Around Here.
Although your poem was accepted
for publication by our journal,
and you signed the contract,
you still must fill out
our routing form, then
walk it through the many offices
of people who must
also sign it in order for it
to be institutionally validated.
You will note on the routing slip
all the places you must trudge
in sequence, and have
all the supervisors sign it
by tomorrow. This will not
be an easy task, but
think of it as following
William Stafford's "golden thread"
to an outcome that can never
be known at the outset
of the journey. Still,
you must try if you want
to have your poem published
in our fine journal.
Good luck!

BLACK SPARKS
   for Juhani Ihanus

Here all sparks are black;
they spit from inner fire,
penetrate the blinding lies of light,
till at last one can see.

They expose to scrutiny
the Pied Piper's fatuous
illumination: "Follow me,
and I will lead you
to the Promised Land,"
a way lit by sun and moon,
incandescence and fluorescence –
to everyone's ruin
except the Piper's.
People follow him
to the edge of a cliff,
then drop into oblivion,
still singing his tune.
He is the only one
to stand his ground.
Who can fault the Pied Piper?
He showed everyone the way;
they could see for themselves
exactly where they were headed.
Few did not join this irresistible march.

The black sparks quietly waited
to salvage what they could
of those who stayed behind.

Better darkness than this light.
Gather the black sparks
and redeem the world.

Sandra Indig, *Warrior*, acrylic on canvas, 38"x32"

DERMATOLOGY

Blacks
Muslims
Latinos
Jews
American Indians
Women
Lesbians
Gays
Bisexuals
Transgenders
Poor folks
Old folks . . . .

Exposed to hate
like skin to decades
of blistering sun,
ripe for basal cell
and squamous cell carcinoma.
No longer protected
by a social skin
of shared belonging –
cast outside the body
of common humanity.

I am one of you,
my kin,
and my skin
erupts with lesions
of fathomless dread.

STEWARDSHIP*

A large convocation of foxes
gathered to consider how to manage
hundreds of chicken coops
and hen houses. The lead fox proclaimed:
"We need the best hen and chicken
managers we can find to fulfill
our fiduciary responsibility."
After days of rumination,
nomination, speeches, and voting,
the best among the foxes
were elected managers
of chicken and hen houses
throughout the land.
Gradually the hen and chicken
population declined in all precincts,
with fewer and fewer coops and houses
to oversee. In this crisis, an emergency
meeting of the supreme council of foxes
soon discovered that their appointees
were eating those in their charge.
More time passed, and the depleted
houses were now empty of inhabitants.
At the next council meeting,
the wise supreme leader calmed
his fellow foxes with a wink of his eye,
saying, "You know, foxes will be foxes,"
whereupon the council set out to find
other, new, untapped precincts
of hens and chickens
over which to exercise their

sacred stewardship
until the last hen and chicken
had disappeared.

*This poem in the form of a parable was written on the day, early in the presidency of Donald Trump, when Scott Pruitt was confirmed as the head of the EPA.

Sandra Indig, *Doubling the Life*,
acrylic on canvas, 17"x13"

Sandra Indig, *Ghost of Stone*,
acrylic on archival paper, 11"x14"

WELCOME

Welcome to the land
of no hope, but dread;
of no listening, but shouting;
of no love, but hate;
of no safety, but cowering.
Welcome to the unwelcoming land,
where trust is shipwrecked
on the craggy shoals
of bitterness and revenge.

Good morning to a bloody sun;
good evening to a crimson moon;
and good night to weeping stars.
The universe no longer knows
what to make of us –
nor do we, as every stranger
fears assault from those
who feel assaulted
by every kind of stranger.

Who will extend
the first arm of reconciliation,
to bridge the trenches
we have dug
with our shovels of contempt?
The hour is late,
but dawn is always possible.

PERMISSIONS

PERMISSIONS
FOR PREVIOUSLY PUBLISHED POEMS

Note: Many journals and literary magazines in which these poems were originally published are no longer in existence. Permissions were therefore not possible, and only the full citation was given. With many journals and literary magazines, copyright reverted to the author after first publication; thus permission was not needed.

AFTER YOU DIED
Originally published in 2016, in *DoveTales: Family and Cultural Identity. An International Journal of the Arts*. Ft. Collins, CO: Writing for Peace (p. 402).
Reprinted with permission.

A LITTLE MORNING MUSIC UNDER STALIN
Originally published in 2015, in *Clio's Psyche*, *21*(4), 472-473.
Reprinted with permission.

ARITHMETIC
Originally published in 2018, by voxpoetica.com.
Retrieved on April 1, 2018 from
http://voxpoetica.com/arithmetic/.

BEFORE SANDIA MOUNTAIN, NM
Originally published in 2015, in *DoveTales: Nature, An International Journal of the Arts*. Ft. Collins, CO: Writing for Peace (p. 93).
Reprinted with permission.

BEHOLDING
Originally published in 2016, in *miller's pond, 9*(3).

Retrieved on August 27, 2016 from
http://www.millerspondpoetry.com/index.php/issues/web_editions1/vol9_2web/vol19web3-3#HowardF.Stein

BLACK SPARKS
Originally published in 2014, in *miller's pond*, *17*(3).
Retrieved on August 24, 2014 from
http://www.millerspondpoetry.com/index.php/issues/index.php?page=vol-17-web-3#HowardF.Stein

BODY HUNGER
Originally published in 2016, in *Pulse – Voices at the Heart of Medicine*.
Retrieved on May 6, 2016 from
http://pulsevoices.org/index.php/archive/poems/747-body-hunger

BOXES EVERYWHERE
Originally published in 2016, in *Friday's Poems/Ascent Aspirations Magazine*.
Retrieved on September 2, 2016 from
http://www.davidpfraser.ca/fridays-poems.html

BRISTLECONE PINE, GREAT BASIN
Originally published in 2016, by *High Plains Society for Applied Anthropology*.
Retrieved on July 25, 2016 from
http://hpsfaa.org/resources/Pictures/2016-07-25_0917.png.
Republished in 2016, in *Friday's Poems/Ascent Aspirations Magazine*.
Retrieved on December 16, 2016 from
http://www.davidpfraser.ca/fridays-poems.html.

PERMISSIONS

CHARACTER
Originally published in 2013 by American Indian Diabetes Prevention Center, in *AIDPC Connections*, *1*(4), 3.

COMPANY MAN
Originally published in 2015, by Center for the Study of Organizational Change, University of Missouri, Columbia, MO.
Retrieved on April 28, 2015 from
http://csoc.missouri.edu/company-man/.

CONTRADICTIONS
Originally published in 2015 (as the Poem of the Day), in *Songs of Eretz Poetry Review,16*.
Retrieved on December 16, 2015 from
http://www.songsoferetz.com/2015/12/poem-of-day-contradictions-by-howard-f.html.

CROCUS IN WINTER
Originally published in 2017, in *vox poetica*.
Retrieved on February 13, 2017 from
http://voxpoetica.com/crocus-winter/.

DEDICATION
Originally published in 2014, in H. F. Stein (2014), *Raisins and Almonds* (p.2). Georgetown, KY: Finishing Line Press.

DERMATOLOGY
Originally published in 2017, in *Journal of Psychohistory*, 45(2), 147.
Reprinted with permission.

DOWNSIZING
Originally published in 2007, in *Harp-Strings Poetry Journal, 18*(4), 18-19.

EMBRACES
Originally published in 2017, by *vox poetica*.
Retrieved on July 25, 2017 from
http://voxpoetica.com/embraces/.

FILLING IN
Originally published in 2017, in *Friday's Poems/Ascent Aspirations Magazine*.
Retrieved on February 24, 2017 from
http://www.davidpfraser.ca/fridays-poems.html.

GOOD ENOUGH
Originally published in 2015, in *The Applied Anthropologist*, 35(2), 56.
Reprinted with permission.

HANDS
Originally published in 2017, by *vox poetica*.
Retrieved on September 26, 2017 from
http://voxpoetica.com/hands/.

HOW THINGS WORK AROUND HERE
Originally published in 2014, in *The Applied Anthropologist, 34*(1-2), 42.
Reprinted with permission.

IN THE CROSS HAIRS
Originally published in 2015, in *miller's pond poetry*, 18(3), web edition.

PERMISSIONS

Retrieved on September 1, 2015 from
http://www.millerspondpoetry.com/index.php/issues/index
php?page=vol18web3#Howard F. Stein.

KEEPING THE LAWN TRIMMED, OR HOW I
BECAME A BETTER CITIZEN
Originally published in 2011, in *Harp-Strings Poetry Journal, 23*(1), 15-16.

KEYS
Originally published in 2011, in *Harp-Strings Poetry Journal, 22*(3), 19.

LEAVING GHOST RANCH, NM
Originally published in 2017, by *vox poetica*.
Retrieved on March 26, 2017 from
http://voxpoetica.com/leaving-ghost-ranch-nm/.

MESAS AND MEADOWS, GHOST RANCH, NM
Originally published in 2017, by *vox poetica*.
Retrieved on January 12, 2017 from
http://voxpoetica.com/mesas-meadows.

MESAS AND MOUNTAINS, GHOST RANCH, NM
Originally published in July 2017; *Friday's Poems/Ascent Aspirations Magazine*.
Retrieved on July 8, 2017 from
http://www.davidpfraser.ca/fridays-poems.html.

METRIC
Originally published in Spring 2014, in *miller's pond* 17(2).

Retrieved on May 15, 2014 from
http://www.millerspondpoetry.com/index.php/issues/index.php?page=vol-17-web-2#HowardF.Stein.

MYCOPLASMA WINTER
Originally published in 2014, in *Blood and Thunder: Musings on the Art of Medicine*, 2014, *14*, 66. Oklahoma City, OK: University of Oklahoma College of Medicine.

NIGHTFALL AT GHOST RANCH, NM
Originally published in 2017, in *Friday's Poems/Ascent Aspirations Magazine*.
Retrieved from http://www.davidpfraser.ca/fridays-poems.html.
Reprinted in 2017, in *miller's pond* (20), web1 edition.
Retrieved on February 10, 2017 from:
http://www.millerspondpoetry.com/index.php/issues/index.php?page=vol20web1#Howard F. Stein

PALPABLE
Originally published in 2017, in *vox poetica*.
Retrieved on June 1, 2017 from
http://voxpoetica.com/palpable/.

PLANETARY
Originally published in 2016, by *vox poetica*.
Retrieved on November 5, 2016 from
http://voxpoetica.com/planetary/.

PRESSED LEAF
Originally published in 2012, in *Oklahoma Today*, 62(6), 93.
Reprinted with permission.

PERMISSIONS

PURPOSE
Originally published in 2017, in *vox poetica*.
Retrieved on June 26, 2017 from
http://voxpoetica.com/purpose/.

RECKONING TIME, GHOST RANCH, NM
Originally published in 2017, in *Friday's Poems/Ascent Aspirations Magazine*.
Retrieved on August 25, 2017 from
http://www.davidpfraser.ca/fridays-poems.html.

RECOGNITION
Originally published in 2013 as RECOGNITION: A HISTORIC FANTASY in *Forensic Psychiatry*.
Retrieved on February 3, 2013 from http://www.forensic-psych.com/articles/artRecognitionAHistoricalFantasy.php.
Reprinted with permission from Dr. Harold J. Bursztajn.

REDEMPTION FROM THE EARTH
Originally published in 2016, in *miller's pond*, 9(3).
Retrieved on August 27, 2016 from
http://www.millerspondpoetry.com/index.php/issues/web_editions1/vol9_2web/vol19web3-3#-3HowardF.Stein.
Republished in 2016, in *Journal of Psychohistory*, 44(2), 136.

REFUGEES
Originally published in 2016, in *Anthropology Now*, 8(1), 46.
Reprinted by permission of Taylor & Francis Ltd.

SLASH AND BURN
Originally published in 2017, by *vox poetica*.

Retrieved on April 24, 2017 from
http://voxpoetica.com/shash-burn/.

STEWARDSHIP
Originally published in 2017, in *Journal of Psychohistory* 45(2), 148.
Reprinted with permission.

SURVIVOR'S WOUND
Originally published in 2014, in *International Psychoanalysis*.
Retrieved on April 7, 2014 from http://internationalpsychoanalysis.net/category/poetry/.

THE BOX
Originally published in 2015, in *Floyd County Moonshine*, 7(2), 64-65.

THE CELLIST
Originally published in 2014, by Broken Tree Press.
Retrieved on January 24, 2014 from http://www.brokentreepress.com/Stein%20Poems.html

THE CORPORATE TABLE
Originally published in 2015 by *The Applied Anthropologist*, 35(1), 39.
Reprinted with permission.

TRIUMPH OF HATE
Originally published in 2016, by *vox poetica*.
Retrieved on December 5, 2016 from http://voxpoetica.com/triumph-hate/.

PERMISSIONS

TWEET AND TEXT
Originally published in 2017, by *vox poetica*.
Retrieved on August 25, 2017 from
http://voxpoetica.com/tweet-text/.

UNCLE HYMEN
Originally published in 2013, in *Accredited Psychiatry and Medicine*.
Retrieved on February 25, 2013 from http://www.forensic-psych.com/articles/artUncleHymen.php.
Reprinted with permission from Dr. Harold J. Bursztajn.

VOID, GHOST RANCH, NM
Originally published in 2017, in *Friday's Poems/Ascent Aspirations Magazine*.
Retrieved on September 16, 2017 from
http://www.davidpfraser.ca/fridays-poems.html.

WELCOME
Originally published in 2017, by *What Rough Beast/Indolent Books*.
Retrieved on February 27, 2017 from
http://www.indolentbooks.com/what-rough-beast-poem-for-february-27-2017/.
Republished in 2017; *Journal of Psychohistory, 45*(2), 148.
Reprinted with permission.

WITHOUT WINDOWS, WITHOUT LIGHT
Originally published in H. F. Stein (2001), *Nothing personal, just business: A guided journey into organizational darkness* (p. vii). Westport, CT: Quorum Books. Out of print.

WHERE IS THE BLOOD?
Originally published in 2017, in *Anthropology Now, 9*(1), 139.
Reprinted with permission of Taylor and Francis, Ltd.

WINTER STRAW
Originally published in 2015, in *Harp-Strings Poetry Journal, 26*(3), 15.

ON A PERSONAL NOTE,
OR A FEW WORDS ABOUT THE AUTHOR

Howard F. Stein is Professor Emeritus in the Department of Family and Preventive Medicine, University of Oklahoma Health Sciences Center (Oklahoma City, OK), where he taught from 1978 to 2012. Dr. Stein is a poet, psychohistorian, and an applied, psychoanalytic, medical, and organizational anthropologist. When he took a teaching position and moved to Oklahoma in 1978, he fell in love with rural wheat farming culture and rural medicine, both of which find expression in his clinical and scholarly books, as well his poetry. In 2006, he was nominated for Oklahoma Poet Laureate, and is currently Poet Laureate of the High Plains Society for Applied Anthropology.

Howard Stein also greatly enjoys "facilitating" organizational groups as part of his consulting. Between 2012 and 2017, he was the group process facilitator with the American Indian Diabetes Prevention Center in Oklahoma City, OK. In late 2015, he published a book of stories from organizational life and psychodynamic analyses, with Dr. Seth Allcorn (senior author), a former long-time health sciences center executive. The book is titled *The Dysfunctional Workplace* (Univ. of Missouri Press). Also, the 2nd edition of Howard's 1994 book, *Listening Deeply*, was published in 2017 (Univ. of Missouri Press). Howard's new book of poetry, *Light and Shadow*, was published in late 2016 (Doodle and Peck Publishing). Some other books of poems written by Howard Stein are: *Evocations*; *Learning Pieces*; *Sketches on the Prairie*; *From My Life, Theme and Variations*; *In the Shadow of Asclepius*; *Seeing Rightly with the Heart*; and *Raisins and Almonds*.

Trained originally in historical musicology, Howard Stein spends a lot of time listening to classical music, and enjoys listening to it with his son Zev, whenever his son, a graduate in music education from the University of Science and Arts of Oklahoma, and a fantastic drummer who plays in several local groups, comes home to visit. Stein also loves to sit outside on his little front porch among the blackjack scrub oak trees.

Howard Stein can be reached at howard-stein@ouhsc.edu or 405-787-6074.

IMMERSE...

Tchaikovsky, *Meditation, Op.42, No.1*, fragment of musical notation

IMMERSE...

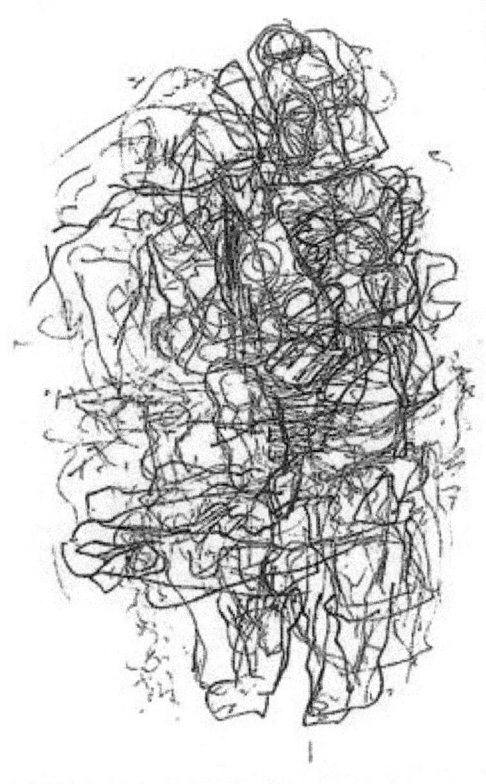

Sandra Indig, *Woman of the Bible No.9*,
charcoal on paper, 14''x10''

www.ingramcontent.com/pod-product-compliance
Lightning Source LLC
Chambersburg PA
CBHW050639160426
43194CB00010B/1733